# TABLE OF CONTENTS

# BACK TO BASICS: DETAINING OUR ENEMIES IN A CONFUSED LEGAL LANDSCAPE

## Introduction

*It used to be a simple thing to fight a battle . . . .In a perfect world, a general would get up and say, "Follow me, men," and everybody would say, "Aye, sir," and would run off. But that's not the world anymore . . . [Now] you have to have a lawyer or a dozen.*[1]

> General James L. Jones, U.S. Marine Corps, while Supreme Allied Commander, Europe. General Jones is now retired and currently serving as President Obama's National Security Advisor.

One can only wonder what General (Retired) Jones would say in his current position about the number of lawyers required to fight a battle, much less actually win a war, when the simple issue of detaining our enemies has grown into such a complex and confusing exercise. Perhaps the struggle of U.S. leaders to establish a clear policy for the detention of enemy supporters and fighters in this armed conflict is evidence of Clausewitz's observation that "[E]verything is very simple in war, but the simplest thing is difficult."[2] Throughout much of the history of warfare, those like today's terror suspects who took part in armed conflict without being part of the "uniformed army" were summarily killed when captured.[3] Now, the U.S. finds itself criticized both home and abroad for merely detaining these individuals under humane conditions. A Washington Post editorial calls on the government to craft "a sound legal structure to govern indefinite detentions."[4] But such a legal structure is already in place and indefinite detention is, as will be explained more fully below, a myth.

The U. S. Government itself has contributed to this confusion. The May 2010 National Security Strategy was drafted in such a way that prosecution of suspected terrorist is our first option and, only if they can't be prosecuted, the U.S. we will turn to a system of prolonged detention in order to protect the American people.[5] U.S. officials openly discuss the recidivism rate of former detainees that have been released. This use of criminal law terminology to address what is really a law of war issue adds to the confusion as to whether we are arresting criminals or capturing enemies.[6] A discussion of recidivism would have been simply unimaginable in past conflicts. One has to wonder why U.S. national security officials would find any rate of recidivism acceptable.

One of the consequences of the U.S. failure to provide the courts and the public with a logical legal framework to explain who we are detaining and why, we find ourselves in a position where, from a legal standpoint, it is arguably easier for U.S. forces to kill our enemies than it is to detain them. This should be troubling to leaders and citizens alike. Release of enemies captured during armed conflict is not required by law or common sense until, in the words of the U.S. Court of Appeals for the District of Columbia, "the fighting stops."[7] Under international law, detention is viewed as a lesser form of coercion than even trial, much less death. Doesn't it then logically follow that it should be easier, or at least not more difficult, to detain someone than to kill them?

This paper suggests an approach to handling detainees that is not only lawful and reasonable; it is easily understandable by the average individual on the street. We should call suspected terrorist with connections to al Qaeda, the Taliban or associated forces what they are – our enemies – and detain them under the law of war until the end of this conflict. If any of these detainees committed criminal misconduct prior to their capture, they can be prosecuted in federal court or military commissions, whichever forum is more appropriate under the circumstances.[8]

## A Confusing Mixture

To date the United States has employed a confusing mixture of domestic criminal law and law of war when dealing with detainees. Little time and effort has been put forth in explaining why some detainees are referred to as "law of war" detainees while others are prosecuted under U.S. criminal statutes in federal courts. This absence of a logical explanation has added fuel to arguments such as the often repeated one that charging detainees with crimes in federal court is treating them as "common criminals." This criticism is, in part, valid. They shouldn't be treated *solely* as common criminals. To do so would be using the wrong legal tool to address the real problem, which the Courts, Congress and the President all agree, is the on-going armed conflict with al Qaeda, the Taliban and associated forces.

## Why Detain? Enemy or Criminal?

When involved in armed conflict the reason you detain your enemies is to remove them from the fight until the fight is over. This is a time honored, universally recognized, lawful and logical basis to detain someone. You do not return your enemy to the fight. You are lawfully required to release your enemy only at the end of the conflict be that in ten days, ten months, ten years, or longer. The so called indefinite detention of those captured during the current conflict is no more indefinite that the detention of any combatant (lawful or unlawful) in any prior war. Release from detention under the law of war has always been tied to an event, the end of the conflict, rather than to a date certain. In that sense, law of war detention is always, by definition, indefinite when compared to a specific sentence handed down by a criminal court after conviction of a criminal offense.

This fiction of indefinite detention has influenced even the Supreme Court. The Court's decision in *Boumediene v. Bush*, 128 S.Ct. 2229 (2008), shows the majority was clearly troubled by the length of detention in the current armed conflict. In explaining the rationale for its decision to grant habeas rights to detainees held in Guantanamo, the Court states, "[B]ecause our Nation's past military conflicts have been of limited duration, it has been possible to leave the outer boundaries of war powers undefined." [9] This writer has been unable to locate any authority to support the proposition that U.S. domestic law changes depending on whether a war is viewed as long or short. The law of war does not contain a time element. It either applies, or it doesn't. There should be no issue that the law of war applies here as the Supreme Court determined in one of its earlier detainee case opinions that the conflict with al Qaeda was a non international armed conflict to which Common Article 3 of the Geneva Conventions applied. [10]

The *Boumediene* opinion is also quite puzzling when it acknowledges that in an armed conflict between nation states "[J]udicial intervention might have complicated the military's ability to negotiate exchange of prisoners with the enemy, a wartime practice well known to the Framers." [11] Yet the Court apparently did not see that granting habeas rights to detainees captured in the current conflict would complicate matters for the military going well beyond the issue of prisoner exchanges. One needs only to read the Washington Post article, *As U.S. pursues al-Qaeda, more kills and fewer captures*, [12] to see how mistaken the Court was in that assumption. This article discusses how detentions have become more difficult due to legal concerns. Some intelligence and military officials, according to the article, believe this has lead to a bias in favor of authorizing kills. As a consequence, the U.S. is missing the opportunity to gain valuable intelligence from individuals who are killed instead of being captured. Another recent article echoed this concern noting that "[S]ome Defense officials believe the U.S. is often pushed into trying to kill militants, instead of attempting to capture and question them because there is no prison where these suspects can be held and questioned due to the 'legal and ethical quandaries' surrounding U.S. detention policy."[13]

Criminal law detention serves a completely different purpose from law of war detention. Criminal law's purpose is to punish members of our society for their wrongdoing, usually by confining them for a specified period of time. Release under criminal law is tied to a date certain, the end of the period of adjudged confinement. The purpose of law of war detention is not served by confining someone for a set period of time. As the United States Circuit Court of Appeals, Ninth Circuit, stated "[T]he object of capture is to prevent the captured individual from serving the enemy."[14] You want to deny the enemy manpower in order to bring the conflict to an end. A policy that employs only criminal prosecution during an armed conflict would not be in national security interest of the United States.

Charging these individuals with violations of criminal law while ignoring their connection to, and association with, our enemies, al Qaeda, the Taliban, or associated forces, is much like a doctor who treats a patient's symptoms but not the underlying disease. That approach may offer some temporary relief but it does not solve the problem. Even though he admitted receiving the bomb and instructions on how to detonate it from al Qaeda,[15] the indictment of Umar Farouk Abdulmutallab, the attempted Christmas Day bomber on Northwest Flight 253, does not even mention al Qaeda.[16] Think of the problem this way. The U.S. has two issues with Mr. Abdulmutallab it must address; one, he wants to fight the United States as an associate of al Qaeda and two, he allegedly committed a crime by attempting to blow up a U.S.

flagged aircraft in furtherance of that goal. Charging him with crimes addresses only the second issue while completely ignoring the first and arguably more important issue. Once Mr. Abdulmutallab serves his sentence, what then? Release him? If we do, have we done anything to address the real issue?

Compare this with the case of the alleged Somali pirates recently indicted in the Eastern District of Virginia.[17] There has been no allegation that these men are in any way connected to al Qaeda, the Taliban, or any associated group. From all appearances, these eleven individuals wanted to capture a ship, hold it for ransom, and make money. They do not have any political or other agenda. They are common criminals who resorted to crime as a way of supporting themselves. Criminal prosecution is an adequate response to the threat posed by these individuals.

## General Noriega: Enemy, Criminal, or Both?

This is not a new argument or even a particularly novel one. The case of General Manuel Noriega provides an example of how these two bases for detention, criminal law and law of war, can apply to the same individual. There is no legal impediment to holding someone both as a prisoner during armed conflict and as a criminal suspect/sentenced prisoner after a criminal conviction. These are two separate, but not mutually exclusive, theories supporting detention.

Captured by U.S. forces during the invasion of Panama in 1989, General Noriega was turned over to agents of the Drug Enforcement Administration for prosecution on various drug offenses. General Noriega had been indicted on these offenses prior to U.S. military action against Panama. Consequently, at the time of his capture, the U.S. could detain General Noriega under two legal theories 1) as a prisoner of war due to his position as head of the Panamanian Defense Force and 2) as an indicted criminal facing federal criminal charges. During his

6

prosecution, General Noriega raised the claim that he was entitled to the rights of a prisoner of war and that this status deprived the Court of jurisdiction to proceed with the criminal case against him.[18] The District Court held that, assuming he was entitled to prisoner of war treatment, his prosecution on various drug offenses was not barred.[19]

After his conviction of drug offenses, General Noriega again raised the issue of his prisoner of war status, this time in relation to where he could be incarcerated as he served his criminal sentence. The District Court held that General Noriega was "in fact a prisoner of war as defined by Geneva III and must be afforded the protections established by the treaty."[20] However, after an extensive review of the relevant provisions of Geneva III, the court went on to find that General Noriega could be held in a civilian prison "so long as he is afforded the full benefits of the Convention."[21] So even though the U.S. could no longer hold General Noriega as a prisoner of war once the fighting had stopped in Panama, it could continue to hold him pending his trial on criminal charges. Once convicted, the U.S. lawfully continued to hold General Noriega as a sentenced prisoner.

Prior to completing his criminal prison sentence in the U.S., France requested General Noriega's extradition to face criminal charges in that country. General Noriega filed a petition for a writ of habeas corpus challenging his extradition. He argued that his extradition to France would violate the Third Geneva Convention in a number of respects. He argued that as a prisoner of war, he could not be transferred to French custody but must be immediately released and repatriated to Panama. He also argued that, in accordance with the Geneva Conventions, if he were transferred the U.S. must first get assurances from France that he would continue to be treated as a prisoner of war.

The United States Court of Appeals for the Eleventh Circuit did not find these arguments persuasive.[22] Although it found that section 5 of the Military Commissions Act precluded General Noriega from invoking the Geneva Conventions as a source of rights in a habeas proceeding, it went on to address his substantive claims. The court held that the United States had fully complied with its legal obligations under the Geneva Conventions and that the Geneva Convention does not prevent the extradition of a prisoner of war. The court cited Article 119 of the Third Geneva Convention to support its position. Although prisoners of war are normally required to be released "without delay after the cessation of active hostilities," Article 119 does allow for prisoners who are facing criminal proceedings to be detained until the end of those proceedings, and, if convicted, until the completion of punishment.[23]

The U.S. Supreme Court denied General Noriega's petition for a writ of certiorari from the Eleventh Circuit's opinion although two justices (Justice Thomas joined by Justice Scalia) dissented. The dissenters argued that the court should grant the petition as the court's opinion would "help the political branches and the courts discharge their responsibilities over detainee cases."[24]

If an individual detainee such as General Noriega who is entitled to the protections of the Geneva Conventions as a prisoner of war, the highest level of protection any detained person can receive, can be prosecuted for criminal offenses, then certainly those detained in the current armed conflict not meriting that same level of protection can be prosecuted as well. If the courts found that it is not "mutually exclusive" to be a prisoner of war and a criminal suspect/convicted felon, there should be no legal issue with being a law of war detainee in the current armed conflict and a criminal suspect at the same time.[25]

## Importance of the Individual

The Authorization for Use of Military Force (AUMF) is a reflection of the fact that Congress and the President knew this conflict would differ from those of the past. For the first time, Congress authorized the use of force against "organizations or persons," in addition to nations.[26] In a filing in U.S. District Court for the District of Columbia on March 13, 2009, the Department of Justice defined the scope of U.S. detention authority under AUMF as follows:

> The President has the authority to detain persons that the President determines planned, authorized, committed, or aided the terrorist attacks that occurred on September 11, 2001, and persons who harbored those responsible for those attacks. The president also has the authority to detain persons who were part of, or substantially supported, Taliban or al Qaida forces or associated forces that are engaged in hostilities against the United States or its coalition partners, including any person who has committed a belligerent act, or has directly supported hostilities, in aid of such enemy armed forces.[27]

In this fight, we have to understand that a single individual may well be an associated force. In fact that is a fitting way to think of these individuals that either through some sort of recruitment or self identification come to associate with al Qaeda to plan, attempt, or actually carry out various attacks. The September 11th attacks were carried out by 19 individuals, the London transit bombings were carried out by four individuals, the shoe bomber, Richard Reed, and Flight 253 bomber, Abdulmutallab, were single individuals. There will be no future set piece battles against al Qaeda formations in the field. The lone individual may well become (if it's not already) our enemy's primary force for carrying out attacks. Because of this choice of tactics, we must exercise even more care in dealing with each individual suspected of terrorist involvement and connection to our enemies, al Qaeda, the Taliban or other associated groups, than we have in past conflicts.

## Confusion in U.S. Policy

The following exchange between the Attorney General and David Gregory of NBC news during the Attorney General's May 9, 2010 interview on the NBC news program "Meet the Press" illustrates how people do not understand there are two different bases for detention. This exchange occurred after the Attorney General stated that Khalid Sheik Mohammed would not be released into the U.S. if he was acquitted at trial.

> MR. GREGORY: So, if he's acquitted, he would not be released. How is that consistent, Mr. Attorney General, with fairness and justice that you believe in of our system?
> MR. HOLDER: Well, he certainly would be provided fairness and justice with regard to the trial that would occur. And with regard to the outcome of that trial, we have – if— and if he were acquitted, what I was trying to say that there are other mechanisms that we have that we might employ, immigration laws that we could use, the possibility of detaining him under the laws of war. There are a variety of things that we can do in order to protect the American people, and that is the thing that I keep uppermost in my mind.
> MR. GREGORY: But, but if he's acquitted and the United States says we will not let him free, then what is the point of having a trial?
> MR. HOLDER: Well, there are other charges that are – that could be brought against him in addition to those he would stand accused of with regard to the 9/11 plot. There are a variety of other things that he could be tried for. And I think we can provide him with fairness and with justice in the systems that we now have in place.[28]

Although the *possibility* of law of war detention is buried in the Attorney General's response, a better approach would be to clearly explain that law of war detention is a basis for detaining Khalid Sheik Mohammed. While he is detained under this basis, he may be tried for pre-capture offenses that violate U.S. law. Even if found "not guilty" of these offenses, he would still continue to be detained not as a convicted criminal, but as someone who falls within the definition of a detainable individual under the Authorization for Use of Military Force and the laws of war. Mr. Gregory's question above shows that he does not understand this argument and believes that the only reason the United States has for detaining Khalid Sheik Mohammed is that he is a criminal suspect.

The short-comings of favoring criminal prosecution to the exclusion of law of war detention are highlighted by the case of Ali Saleh Kahlah al-Marri. After being detained for over seven years, al-Mari was indicted in federal court on two counts of providing material support to terrorist, specifically al-Qaeda. He plead guilty to both charges admitting that he attended al-Qaeda training camps. He also admitted that he came to the U.S. at the direction of Khalid Sheikh Mohammed and was told to await further instructions. After stating at sentencing that he no longer desired to attack the U.S., al-Mari was sentenced to eight years and four months confinement.[29] At the end of this period of confinement (with sentence credit for good time he'll probably serve only five years) what happens to al-Marri? Does the U.S. release him? If he is a common criminal, that course of action would make sense. But if we are at war and he is a part of or associated with our enemy, it makes absolutely no sense to release him. His release is not required by the law of war. The criminal law basis for detaining Al-Mari will have been satisfied when he completes his sentence but the law of war basis remains.

To date, our application of both military commissions and criminal laws in the current conflict has ignored this very basic distinction between the laws of war and criminal law. Those convicted of law of war violations by military commissions were not legally required to be released at the end of their sentences. The U.S. certainly could release the individuals for political, foreign policy or other reasons but it was not legally required to do so. If these convicted individuals were in fact combatants, either legal or illegal, they can lawfully be detained until the end of the conflict. A defense official involved in negotiations that led to Salim Ahmed Hamdan, Osama bin Laden's former driver, being returned to his home in Yemen to serve the remainder of his military commission sentence was quoted as saying "Legally, we absolutely have a right to hold enemy combatants, but politically is he the guy we want to fight all the way to the Supreme Court about? I think we came to the conclusion that, no, he wasn't."[30] However, actions like the return of Hamdan have not been sufficiently explained so that the public understands that the U.S was not legally required to take that course of action.

Confusion in U.S. Courts

The intervention of the courts has not brought clarity to this issue. If anything it has added another layer of uncertainty and further complicated the war effort of the United States. Courts have become the driving force in an issue that is better suited for resolution by the political branches. Even the Supreme Court appears to acknowledge this. As noted earlier, the Court recognized in *Boumediene* that "judicial intervention might have complicated the military's ability to negotiate exchanges of prisoners with the enemy, a wartime practice well know to the Framers,"[31] in the context of a declared war between nations states. If anything, the courts invention in detainee cases has complicated this issue even more under the circumstances of the current non-international armed conflict than it would have if this was a war between nation states and thus, a more traditional international armed conflict. In everything from negotiating with other countries to resettle detainees, to trying to reach accommodation with some warring factions, the Executive Branch must now also be concerned about what the courts will do as it tries to resolve these issues. Our enemies are aware of the courts involvement. Individual detainees may see the courts as a potential escape value and consequently be unwilling to entertain any approaches on reconciliation and cooperation by U.S. officials. Our enemies are able to monitor court proceedings and learn from them.

As the number of court challenges grow, it has become clearer to all, including the judiciary, that courts are ill suited to determine who is an enemy of the United States. These issues of national security and war are best resolved by the political branches, the popularly elected legislative and executive branches of our government. These two branches have greater access to all available, relevant information without regard to the formal rules of evidence or concerns about what can be released to the detainee without endangering national security. Yet courts have now become the branch of government most heavily engaged in the business of crafting detention policy, one detainee at a time. Nothing illustrates this better than the following excerpt from a detainee case:

> "Regrettably, these unique cases require the Court to make, rather than apply and interpret law. The Supreme Court in *Boumediene* and *Hamdi* charged this court and others with the unprecedented task of developing rules to review the propriety of military actions during a time of war, relying on common law tools. . . . .The common law process depends on incrementalism and eventual correction, and it is most effective where there are a significant number of cases brought before a large set of courts, which in turn enjoy the luxury of time to work the doctrine supple. None of these factors exist in the Guantanamo context. . . [T]he circumstances that frustrate the judicial process are the same ones that make this situation particularly ripe for Congress to intervene pursuant to its policy expertise, democratic legitimacy, and oath to uphold and defend the Constitution."[32]

In addition, it has likely been the courts' involvement in this issue that has lead to the urgency about prosecution and fed the confusion about so-called indefinite detention. Some decision makers may have gotten the mistaken impression that we must either try detainees or release them.  This would be true if the only reason for holding these individuals was their status as criminal suspects.  Again, there is a failure to recognize the law of war basis for detention.

A recent decision of the United States Court of Appeals for the District of Columbia Circuit, *Maqaleh v. Gates, 2010 U.S. App. LEXIS 10384* (2010),  is evidence that the courts are beginning to acknowledge and appreciate some of the challenges we face in fighting the current conflict.  In declining to extend the writ of habeas corpus to detainees held in Bagram Air Force Base, Afghanistan, the Court noted the practical difficulties of applying the writ to aliens captured overseas and being held in an active theater of war.  The Court quoted favorably from the Supreme Court's decision in *Johnson v. Eisentrager*, 339 U.S. 763 (1950) that

> Such trials would hamper the war effort and bring aid and comfort to the enemy.  They would diminish the prestige of our commanders, not only with enemies but with wavering neutrals.  It would be difficult to devise more effective fettering of a field commander than to allow the very enemies he is ordered to reduce to submission to call him to account in his own civil courts and divert his efforts and attention from the military offensive abroad to the legal defensive at home.  Nor is it unlikely that the result of such enemy litigiousness would be a conflict between judicial and military opinion highly comforting to enemies of the United States.[33]

Although written some sixty years ago, these words still ring true.  To quote the Supreme Court opinion in *Boumediene,* "[R]emote in time it may be, irrelevant to the present it is not."[34] In fact, these very real, practical concerns are even more relevant to the current ongoing armed conflict than they were in 1950 occupied Germany.  Today, the U.S. homeland itself is under attack in ways that were not even envisioned in 1950.  Although the *Boumediene* court quoted favorably *Eisentrager's* concern about not wanting to interfere with the military's efforts to contain "enemy elements, guerilla fighters and were-wolves" in post war Germany it inexplicably does not seem to share those concerns for our current effort to contain active fighters in an ongoing armed conflict. Courts thus far have only accepted that we are at war in foreign lands and fail to acknowledge the challenges we face at home. Is this a result of our legal system failing to recognize the tactics of an adaptable enemy? Or is this just another symptom of treating suspected terrorist solely as a criminal justice problem and not acknowledging the law of war part of the equation? Whatever the reason, a well articulated U.S. detention policy explaining that we are detaining individuals under the law of war and that this a separate basis for detention regardless of any prosecution would hopefully assist the courts as they address these issues.

<u>The Battlefield</u>

Defining the battlefield has proven difficult in this conflict. However that term ends up being defined, geographic location at time of capture should not be the determining factor in whether someone is found to be a criminal defendant or an enemy combatant. Under the AUMF as interpreted by the courts, the standard for detainability is whether someone is a member of, or substantially supported, al Qaeda, the Taliban, or an associated force.[35] But some court opinions would lead one to believe that the caution from *Eisentrager* about "calling the field commander to account in his own civil courts" only applies if the enemy is captured and confined outside the U.S.[36] It appears the courts have failed to appreciate the international geographic reach of this armed conflict. There can be little doubt that our enemies take comfort, as the *Eisentrager* opinion warned, in the constant and very public arguing back and forth on how to handle our enemies when they are captured. It must appear to the rest of the world, and U.S. citizens for that matter, that our leaders do not understand our own legal system.

A recent decision of the Court of Appeals for the District of Columbia Circuit highlights another interesting point. In *Al-Bihani v. Obama,* 590 F.3d 866 (2010), the court noted that although detention authority logically includes those individuals who are subject to military commission authority, "detention authority in fact sweeps wider."[37] The *Al-Bihani* opinion is striking in that it is not only well supported by law but grounded in reality as well. The Court recognized that "Detention of aliens outside the sovereign territory of the United States during wartime is a different and peculiar circumstance."[38] The court also acknowledged the potential to compromise military operations if the detention process required military commanders to be concerned with evidentiary standards on the battlefield.[39]

Courts however continue to view the battlefield as being a specific geographic space in some far off land. Have they forgotten that the acts of war that began this armed conflict were attacks at the center of New York City and Washington, D.C.?[40] Attacks which were carried out by individuals dressed as civilians. This is our enemy. This is how they fight, and, as recent failed attacks have shown, how they will continue to fight. There will be no Taliban or al Qaeda invasion fleet that appears over the horizon ready to strike the U.S. homeland although that is the type of enemy Courts continue to envision. These terrorist fighters have been described as "criminals in combat."[41] That is the way we should think of them, regardless of the place of capture. They are not true civilians. They are not common criminals. They are enemy fighters that can lawfully be detained under the laws of war. It should be remembered that those fighters captured within the United States are the al Qaeda and Taliban forces most likely to inflict real harm on the United States.

## Designation of Enemies

One basic question one has to ask is which branch of government is best suited to determine who are enemies of the United States? The Judiciary which considers only evidence admissible under the Federal Rules of Evidence? Or the Executive branch with its superior sources of intelligence and information? One of the basic tenants of the law of war is distinction.[42] In other words, we must distinguish between combatants and civilians and target only combatants. Thus, in order to target someone, commanders are lawfully required to determination that they are a combatant. Shouldn't this determination also be sufficient to detain? The answer is obvious. Yet the courts in this conflict have continued the "unprecedented task of developing rules to review the propriety of military actions during a time of war."[43] Commanders considering whether to target (kill or capture) a suspected enemy combatant consider all relevant information available. Based on their evaluation of the reliability of that information, commanders then decide on whether to target the suspected individual. The Courts, however, only examine admissible evidence under the Federal Rules of Evidence. This is a different standard that can easily lead to drastically different decisions.

*El-Shifa v. United States,* 2010 U.S. App. LEXIS 11585, provides an explanation of why courts take such different positions when it comes reviewing various military actions taken by the President. *El-Shifa* challenged President Clinton's cruise missile strike against a chemical plant in the Sudan in 1998 whose owner was allegedly linked to Osama Bin Laden. The plant owner, Mr. Idris, contented that he was not associated with bin Laden and that his plant was a pharmaceutical plant, not a chemical weapons plant. He sought compensation for the damages to his plant and his reputation. On appeal, the Court of Appeals for the District of Columbia held that this was a non-justicable "political question." The court stated that there was no "constitutional commitment to the courts for review of a military decision to launch a missile at a foreign target"[44] The court distinguished this decision from those on detainees and asset seizures where the courts have found a constitutional commitment to the judiciary. However legally well founded these positions may be, they leave U. S. leaders in the strange position of knowing that their decisions to target and kill someone cannot be challenged in the courts but courts will entertain challenges to their decisions to capture and detain someone.[45]

## A Suggested Approach

We can bring some clarity to this situation by a shift of focus in the approach put forth in the May 2010 National Security Strategy. The current practice of defaulting to a civilian criminal approach and then, only if it appears this course of action will not be successful, holding the detainee into what is referred to as prolonged detention should be abandoned. It's not surprising that this approach raises fears of indefinite detention and confusion about these perpetrators being common criminals. The U.S. should adopt the exact opposite approach. That is, as soon as investigators identify a link between a suspect and "al Qaeda, the Taliban, or associated forces," that suspect should be treated as a law of war detainee. If they are our enemies, and the President, Congress, and the Courts all agree that individuals associated with these groups are, then they should receive the legal treatment that status earns them. [46]

In other words, law of war detention should be a starting point rather than a last resort for those terror suspects with connections to al Qaeda, the Taliban or associated groups. These individuals can be lawfully detained on that basis alone. There is no element of punishment in law of war detention. If investigation turns up sufficient evidence of criminal wrongdoing, then the detained individuals can be prosecuted for that as well. But there is no requirement for a rush to prosecution or for any prosecution at all.

## Role of Civilian Authorities

Adopting this approach to first emphasize the Law of detention authority over any suspect connected to al Qaeda, the Taliban or an associated force does not drastically change the role of civilian authorities. It doesn't mean that civilian law enforcement cannot interrogate suspected terrorist. It doesn't mean suspected terrorist can't be held in civilian confinement facilities. It also doesn't mean that suspect terrorist will not end up facing prosecution in civilian courts. In appropriate cases, they should face civilian prosecution for their crimes. It must be remembered that we are talking about two separate bases for detention. As the case of General Noriega shows, someone does not become immune from criminal prosecution just because they are detained during an armed conflict. Furthermore, they may continue to be lawfully detained until the reasons for their detention under both theories, criminal law and the law of war, have been satisfied.

The military is not trained or staffed to handle internal threats. Nor are they the first line of defense against internal threats under the law. One need only review the Posse Comitatus Act[47] to be reminded that there are criminal consequences if the military is involved in activities that could be considered domestic law enforcement. As a practical matter, who could have airport officials in Detroit called in December 2009 if they wanted Abdulmutallab, the Flight 253 bomber, to be taken into custody by the military? The military does not have a presence in all or even most communities in our nation. It is civilian authorities that will almost always be the first to encounter suspected terrorist. Once individuals are captured, they are most likely to be held in civilian confinement facilities. The military has greatly reduced the number of military confinement facilities over the last 20 years to the point where many military installations must rely upon local civilian confinement facilities to hold their own military suspects requiring confinement.

A great deal of discussion and political posturing has popped up on the issue of Miranda warnings for terror suspects. Whether Miranda is an issue or not depends upon which basis of confinement we are talking about. Miranda plays no part in law of war detention. We do not need to worry about evidence to use at trial in law of war detention because no trial is required. Granted, the U.S. will have to defend against habeas petitions but detainee statements have been admitted in those proceedings without Miranda warnings.[48] Where Miranda becomes a concern is in criminal prosecution.

The Attorney General has raised the possibility of seeking legislation to expand the public safety exception to the Miranda Rule in National Security cases. [49] But is there any real need to alter the Miranda Rule if we adopt the law of war approach? Or would the current application of the public safety exception be sufficient to protect the American public? This is yet another issue that arises from the fundamental error in not clearly deciding who these suspects are and what legal regime governs their treatment. Consequently, all these various theories become inter mixed and inter twined and everyone from the courts to counsel and politicians to the public have no clear grasp of what legal theory applies in a particular case. In attempting to address this issue by tweaking the Miranda Rule, we are again just treating a symptom and not dealing directly with the disease.

The events of May 18, 2010 illustrate the confusing mix of language as to whether these individuals are criminals, terrorist or combatants (and therefore enemies of the United States). The Taliban claimed responsibility for attacks that occurred that day in Kabul, Afghanistan and at Bagram Air Base in Afghanistan.[50] Americans (military members and contractors) and

Afghans died in both these attacks. These attacks were part of the ongoing armed conflict between the Taliban and the United States. That same day, U.S. citizen Faisal Shahzad, appeared before a U.S. magistrate in New York for his initial appearance on charges arising from the attempted bombing in New York's Times Square. According to press reports and the statements of U.S. officials, Shahzad has stated that he received bomb making instruction and assistance from the Pakistani Taliban in his attempted bombing.[51] Based on these statements, Shahzad is detainable under the AUMF. Although there is no legal impediment to bringing criminal charges against someone like Shahzad who can be lawfully detained under the law of war; there is also no requirement that criminal charges be brought in order to continue his detention.

Much like the indictment of Umar Farouk Abdulmuttallab, the criminal complaint against Shahzad makes no mention of his connection to the Pakistani Taliban, although it does mention his admission that he received training in bomb making while in Pakistan.[52] At his initial court appearance on May 18, 2010, Shahzad did not oppose the government's request to continue his detention but his court appointed attorney did say that she may later seek Shahzad's release on bond.[53] The concept of "release on bond" does not exist in law of war detention and the fact that Shahzad's defense counsel believes her client can seek his release on bond is further evidence of how these cases are viewed as ordinary criminal matters. The United States would be better served by directly addressing the law of war basis for detention early on in cases of suspected terrorist with ties to al Qaeda, the Taliban, or associated forces. At the first opportunity the U.S. should present the argument that these "criminals in combat" can be detained under the law of war for the duration of the armed conflict. This would remove the inference that can be drawn from current practice that the U.S. resorts to this apparently weaker fallback position only when it does not possess sufficient evidence to proceed with a criminal prosecution.

## Conclusion

Criminal investigators are the first authorities to encounter suspected terrorist, civilian confinement facilities are readily available, and prosecutors and judges are most comfortable dealing with criminal charges. Consequently an understandable default to criminal prosecution of suspected terrorist developed as it is a proven system, fully in place and easily accessible. However understandable this approach may be, it should be recognized for what it is, a partial response to a multifaceted national security issue.

The U.S. can remedy this problem by clearly stating as a matter of law and U.S. policy, suspected terrorist are detainable under the laws of war and the AUMF if they are linked to al Qaeda, the Taliban, or an associated force. They can continue to be detained under this basis until the conflict with these organizations is over. If violations of either the law of war or U.S. criminal statues are found by further investigation, law of war detainees may face criminal prosecution. This prosecution may take place in either federal courts or military commissions depending upon the circumstances of the particular case.

Adopting this approach will not change our legal treatment of those terror suspects with no al Qaeda, Taliban, or associated force connection. Those suspects will continue to be treated solely as criminal suspects. That is the only lawful approach to handling those individuals unless Congress acts to expand the detention authority under the AUMF. Perhaps highlighting this limitation will spur Congress to further action should they question why some terror suspects are not being treated as a law of war detainees.

This will bring much needed clarity to U.S. policy. As the case law supporting this position was primarily developed in the non terror related case of General Noriega, it should avoid much of the political fighting that has followed other attempts to establish U.S. policy on this topic. It is a policy that is easily understandable by the American public and the world audience at large. Finally, it returns U.S. policy to a basic principle; you detain your enemy when you are at war.

## Endnotes

[1] Lyric Wallwork, "A Marine's toughest mission," *Parade Magazine,* Jan, 19, 2003.

[2] Carl von Clausewitz, On War, 164 (Penguin Books, 1968).

[3] Donald A. Wells, The Laws of Land Warfare. A Guide to the U.S. Army Manuals, 126 (Greenwood Press, 1992).

[4] Editorial, *The Gitmo detention dodge*, Wash. Post, June 20, 2010.

[5] National Security Strategy, The White House, May 2010 at pg. 36. This system of detention is not further defined other than to say it will contain "fair procedures and a thorough process of periodic review."

[6] Letter from John Brennan, Assistant to the President for Homeland Security and Counterterrorism, to The Honorable Nancy Pelosi, Speaker of the House of Representatives, 1 February 2010. The letter states that the U.S. Intelligence Community estimates that 20 per cent of the detainees transferred from Guantanamo are confirmed or suspect of resuming terrorist activity after their release.

[7] *Al-Bihani v. Obama,* 590 F.3d 866, 874(D.C. Cir. 2010).

[8] This issue of what crimes should be tried in what forum is beyond the scope of this paper. The focus of this paper is that there is a sound legal argument for detention of terror suspects linked to al Qaeda, the Taliban or other associated forces. This is a completely independent basis for detention that does not rely on the decision on prosecution.

[9] *Boumediene v. Bush*, 128 S.Ct. 2229, 2277 (2008).

[10] *Hamdan v. Rumsfeld,* 548 U.S. 557, 630 (2006).

[11] *Boumediene supra* note 9 at 2249.

[12] Karen DeYoung and Joey Warrick, *As U.S. pursues al-Qaeda, more kills and fewer captures,* Wash. Post, Feb. 14, 2010, page A1.

[13] Julian E. Barnes, *U.S. hopes to share prison with Afghanistan*, L.A. Times, June 9, 2010.

[14] *In re Territo*, 156 F.2d 142, 145 (1946).

[15] Evan Perez and Jay Solomon, *Nigerian Charged in Northwest Bombing Attempt*, Wall St. J., Dec. 27, 2009.

[16] Indictment of Umar Farouk Abdulmutallab issued in the Eastern District of Michigan, Jan. 6, 2010.

[17] Indictment of Mohammed Modin Hasan, et al., issued in the Eastern District of Virginia on Apr. 27, 2010.

[18] *U.S. v. Noriega*, 746 F. Supp 1506 , 1511( S.D. Fl. 1990).

[19] *Id.*

[20] *U.S. v. Noriega*, 808 F. Supp. 791, 796 (S.D. Fl. 1992).

[21] *Id.* at 803.

[22] *Noriega v. Pastrana*, 564 F.3d 1290 (11th Cir. 2009).

[23] Geneva Convention Relative to the Treatment of Prisoners of War (GC III), August 12, 1949, art. 119.

[24] *Noriega v. Pastrana*, 130 S.Ct. 1002 (2010).

[25] *Noriega, supra* note 20 at 799.

[26] P.L. 107-40, 115 Stat. 224 (2001).

[27] IN RE: GUANTANAMO BAY DETAINEE LITIGATION, Respondents' Memorandum Regarding The Government's Detention Authority Relative to Detainees held at Guantanamo Bay, Misc. No. 08-442 (TFH), United States District Court for the District of Columbia, filed Mar. 13, 2009.

[28] *Meet the Press* (NBC television broadcast May 9, 2010). Interview of Attorney General Eric Holder by NBC News Correspondent David Gregory.

[29] Carrie Johnson, *Judge Credits Time Served in Sentencing al-Qaeda aide*, Wash. Post, Oct. 30, 2009.

[30] Josh White and William Branigin, *Hamdan to Be Sent to Yemen*, Wash. Post, Nov. 25, 2008.

[31] *Boumediene, supra* note 9 at 2248.

[32] *Al-Bihani, supra,* note 9 at 881 (Brown, J., concurring). After stating that "these unique cases require the Court to make, rather than apply and interpret, law" this language was cited by the district court in the Memorandum and Order it issued in another detainee case, *Al-Harbi, et al v. Obama.* The District Court referred to the "novel, unprecedented nature of these proceedings."

[33] *Johnson v. Eisentrager* 339 U.S. 763, 779 (1950).

[34] *Boumediene, supra* note 9 at 2277.

[35] There had been a split of opinion among district court judges as to whether the "substantial support" prong was enough to detain someone but that question was recently settled in favor of detainability by the D.C. Circuit Court of Appeals in *Al-Bihani.*

[36] *Eisentrager, supra* note 33.

[37] *Al-Bihani, supra* note 9 at 872.

[38] *Id*. at 877.

[39] *Id.*

[40] The Attorney General referred to the attacks of 9/11 as an act of war and a violation of federal criminal law in his testimony before Congress on November 18, 2009. *Oversight of the Department of Justice: Hearing Before the S. Judiciary Comm.,* 111th Cong. (2009) (statement of Eric Holder, Att'y Gen. of the United States).

[41] Gary D. Solis, The Law of Armed Conflict: International Humanitarian Law in War, 233 (Cambridge University Press, 2010).

[42] This principle appears as "Rule 1" in *Customary International Humanitarian Law, (2005),* a two volume study by The International Committee of the Red Cross. Jean-Marie Henekaerts and Louise Doswald-Beck, *Customary International humanitarian Law, vol. 1:Rules* (Oxford: Oxford University Press, 2005), 3.

[43] *Eisentrager, supra* note 33.

[44] *El-Shifa v. United States,* 2010 U.S. App. LEXIS 11585.

[45] The Executive Summary of a January 22, 2010 Brookings Institute Governance Study entitled *The Emerging Law of Detention, The Guantanamo Habeas Cases as Lawmaking,* notes that the various court decisions on these detainee cases may well impact military activities unrelated to detention including the decision to target individuals with lethal force.

[46] It should be noted that the U.S. Supreme Court in *Hamdi v. Rumsfeld*, 542 U.S. 507, 518 (2004) recognized the lawfulness of this approach, in light of the AUMF. The Court stated that the detention of individuals covered by the AUMF for the "duration of the particular conflict in which they were captured is so fundamental and accepted an incident to war to be an exercise of the 'necessary and appropriate force' Congress has authorized the President to use."

[47] 18 U.S.C. 1385

[48] *Warafi v. Obama*, 2010 U.S. Dist. LEXIS 35340 (2010). This opinion contains a discussion of how summaries of statements made by detainees to interrogators are allowed into evidence in habeas proceedings. The burden is on the party using these statements to show that they are "accurate, reliable, and credible."

[49] *Meet the Press, supra* note 29.

[50] Joby Warrick, *Bomb attack on NATO convoy kills 5 U.S. troops in Kabul*, Wash. Post, May 19, 2010;Atia Abawi, *Nearly a dozen militants dead after Bagram attack*, May 19, 2010, *available at* http://www.cnn.com.

[51] *Meet the Press, supra* note 29.

[52] Complaint filed 4 May 2010 in the Southern District of New York, U.S. v. Shahzad.

[53] William K. Rashbaum and Benjamin Weiser, *Times Square Bombing Suspect Appears in Court*, N.Y. Times, May 18, 2010.